The Fishing Trip

by Karra McFarlane

illustrated by James Cottell

OXFORD
UNIVERSITY PRESS
AUSTRALIA & NEW ZEALAND

It was the first fishing trip of the season for Jay and his dad.

They were going to take a boat out to Palm Bay. They would spend all day together, just Jay and his dad. It was going to be a special trip.

Jay did not want to go. He wanted to stay at home and try to get to the next level of Worm Hole 500.

"Do we have to go today?" Jay asked his dad. "Maybe we should go next weekend instead."

"The weather is perfect and I have already packed everything," said Dad. "You never know, you might even enjoy yourself!"

"Don't forget to wear your life jacket!" Mum called out.

Jay packed his kit and put his life jacket on. He frowned as he climbed into the boat.

"Cheer up," said Dad.

The sun was shining and the sea
was calm.

"This is the perfect spot!" shouted Jay.
Dad made sure the boat was stationary.
Jay began to unpack the fishing kit.

Dad put the hook on the line. Jay added the sinkers until the line began to sink.

Jay's dad had taught him everything he knew about fishing.

All of a sudden, there was a loud knock against the bottom of the boat. The boat rocked from side to side. Then it happened again.

Jay and his dad looked at each other.
Something unusual was happening.

They waited patiently for the boat to rock for a third time. They both stood in the middle of the boat in silence. Nothing happened.

"You look first," said Jay. "It's your boat!"

Dad peered over the side of the boat. He saw a large shadow pass underneath. "The water is making my vision blurry," said Dad. "I can't make out what it is."

"I'll look now," said Jay. He began to edge to the side of the boat.

Jay peered at the shadow. "It's a dolphin. I'm sure of it," he said, pointing at the shadow. "We learned about them at school. It's not unusual for dolphins to swim close to boats."

Dad took a closer look. The dolphin had a piece of plastic caught on its beak.

"It needs our help," said Jay.

Jay leaned over the side of the boat and held the dolphin. With care, Dad pulled the plastic from its beak.

The dolphin swam away as soon as the plastic was off.

"That was amazing!" Jay smiled. "We saved that dolphin."

Jay forgot all about Worm Hole 500. He could not think about anything but the dolphin. He felt on top of the world! He had never felt so proud.

The pair continued on their fishing trip. They talked, they sang and they caught six fish!

"This is the biggest fish I've ever caught," said Jay. He held up the whopper for a photo.

Dad and Jay put all the fish back in the water after they caught them.

The day flew by. It was time to head back to dry land.

23

"Did you have a good day?" asked Mum as they walked in.

"The best day *ever!*" whooped Jay. "We're going again next weekend!"